PEACOCKS

Sandie Lee Books

Peacocks

This medium-size bird is in the pheasant family. It is also called, a peafowl. There are 3 main types of this bird; the African Congo, the Indian and Green peacock. However, they are all thought to have originated in Asia. In some cultures, the peacock is seen as a guardian of royalty. The image of this fowl was engraved on objects (such as thrones) to show its importance. Read on to discover more about this beautiful and awesome bird.

Where in the World?

Did you know in the wild, the peacock can be found in Pakistan, in Southeast Asia and central Africa? In these areas, the peacock will call deserts and savanna lands home. They will also live in very thick forests. Plus, peacocks can be found in zoos and other locations around the world.

The Body of a Peacock

Did you know the peacock is a robust bird? The peacock can weigh from 8.8 pounds to 13 pounds. This bird can measure from 30 inches to 44 inches tall. Its tail feathers alone can measure from 55 to 63 inches long. It also has a long neck and long legs.

Peacock Feathers

Did you know this bird is one of the most beautiful in the world? The feathers of a peacock are bright blue and green and shimmer in the light. The peacock can have up to 200 feathers in his fan (tail). Each feather has a pattern on the end of it that looks like a beautifully colored eye.

The Peacock's Special

Did you know in the mating season, the male peafowl fans out his tail feathers? When the peacock is trying to impress a female, he will spread out his tail feathers. He will also strut around her and shake his tail feathers. These make a rattling sound to help attract the female's attention.

What a Peacock Eats

Did you know the peacock is a ground feeder? This means they hunt and eat food from the ground. Wild peacocks will eat meat and vegetation. They like insects, berries, grains, snakes, scorpions, grass, flower petals and other parts of various plants. Because of this varied diet, the peacock is called, an omnivore.

The Peacock's Stomach

Did you know the peacock has a special organ in its stomach area? This is called, a gizzard. Since peacocks do not have teeth, they will eat small pebbles. These smooth stones go into the peacock's gizzard. When this bird eats food, it goes through its stomach and into the gizzard. Here the food will be broken down, then passed through its intestines.

Peacocks as Prey

Did you know that peacocks have natural predators in the wild? Large cats such as leopards and tigers will hunt both baby and adult peacocks. Smaller animals like the mongoose or even stray dogs will also hunt this bird. Humans have hunted the peacock for its brightly colored plumage. Habitat loss is also another enemy to the peafowl.

Peacock Talk

Did you know the call of the peacock can be very frightening? During the mating season, the peacock will make a loud shrill call. It has been described as being like a woman screaming. Both peacocks and peahens will make a loud call when they are in danger. This is sometimes enough to scare a predator away.

Peacock Mom

Did you know the female peacock is called, a peahen? The peahen is able to start having eggs at the age of two. She will build a nest on the ground in a protected area. She may also dig out a large bowl-shaped hole in the earth to lay her eggs. She can have 10 or more brownish-colored eggs.

Baby Peacock

Did you know a baby peacock is called, a peachick? After 28 days in its egg, the peachick will peck its way out of it. The baby is born with soft fuzzy feathers all over its body. It can be soft shades of brown with markings on its wings. After only one day, the peachick can walk, run and eat food on its own.

The Peacock at Rest

Did you know peacocks can fly? Even though this bird is quite large, it still has the ability to fly. In fact, peacocks will fly up into tall trees for the night. This is called, roosting. Like other species of birds, the peafowl will often sleep with its head tucked under its feathers.

Life of a Peacock

Did you know the peafowl can live to be in its twenties? In the wild and in captivity, a healthy peafowl can live to be around 25 years-old. The peafowl will live in a small group made up of one male and several females and their peachicks. This is called, a harem.

The Indian Peacock

This bird is originally from Asia. It has bright blue feathers covering its head, neck and chest. This peacock will not get his beautiful tail feathers until he is about 5 or 6 years-old. The peahen is brown in color. This species can be seen in zoos around the United States.

Congo Peacock

This species of the peafowl is found in Africa. Unlike other peacocks, this fella does not have the impressive tail plumage. It is smaller and looks more like a pheasant. This peacock has bright blue feathers on his chest and greener feathers on his wings. The crest on his head has shorter feathers.

Quiz

Question 1: What is another name for the peacock?

Answer 1: The peafowl

Question 2: What does the end of the peacock's tail feather resemble?

Answer 2: An eye

Question 3: What special organ in found in the peacock?

Answer 3: A *gizzard*

Question 4: What does the shrill call of the male peacock sound like?

Answer 4: A woman screaming

Question 5: What is it called when the peacock flies into a tree and sleeps for the night?

Answer 5: Roosting

Thank you for checking out another addition from Sandie Lee Books! Make sure to check out Amazon.com for many other great titles.

www.ingramcontent.com/pod-product-compliance
Lightning Source LLC
Chambersburg PA
CBHW050802290526
45792CB00008B/2294